BOWLING

Mark Miller

SHIRE PUBLICATIONS

Published in Great Britain in 2012 by Shire Publications
Ltd, Midland House, West Way, Botley, Oxford OX2 0PH,
United Kingdom.

44-02 23rd Street, Suite 219, Long Island City, NY 11101,
USA.

E-mail: shire@shirebooks.co.uk   www.shirebooks.co.uk

A CIP catalogue record for this book is available from the
British Library.

Shire Library no. 677.   ISBN-13: 978 0 74781 136 7

Mark Miller has asserted his right under the Copyright,
Designs and Patents Act, 1988, to be identified as the
author of this book.

Designed by Tony Truscott Designs, Sussex, UK
and typeset in Perpetua and Gill Sans.

Printed in China through Worldprint Ltd.

12 13 14 15 16   10 9 8 7 6 5 4 3 2 1

COVER IMAGE
Bowling long has been one of the rare games and sports
that can be enjoyed for a lifetime by friends and families.

TITLE PAGE IMAGE
One of bowling's most appealing traits is that it is a true
lifetime sport the whole family can enjoy.

CONTENTS PAGE IMAGE
It's the pins that make bowling truly unique among sports.

ACKNOWLEDGEMENTS
This book would not be possible without the research and
photographic libraries of the International Bowling
Museum and Hall of Fame and United States Bowling
Congress in Arlington, Texas. Special thanks to IBM/HF
Curator Kelli Thomerson, USBC Managing Director of
Communications Jason Overstreet, Graphic Designer
Brock Kowalsky, and Administrative Assistant Stacy
Slawnikowski. I also want to thank my historical mentors,
including former American Bowling Congress
Communications Executive Steve James, former ABC
Public Relations Manager Dave DeLorenzo, former ABC
Executive Director Al Matzelle (my ultimate historian),
and former WIBC Public Relations Director Augie
Karcher. Special thanks go to the late Bruce Pluckhahn, the
IBM/HF's first curator, who was unable to finish his own
bowling history book. Biggest thanks to go my wife Ann
and daughter Kelly, who have always inspired me to be my
best.

Shire Publications is supporting the Woodland Trust, the UK's leading woodland conservation charity, by funding the dedication of trees.

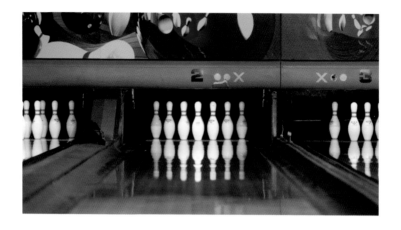

CONTENTS

BOWLING—AMERICA'S INDOOR PASTIME

A T MORE THAN 5,000 years old, bowling may be the world's oldest sport. With more than 100 million annual global participants, it's definitely among the most popular.

Nearly every person in the United States from age 3 to 103 has tried bowling at least once in their lives. More than 70 million partake annually. It's a true lifetime sport that's passed on from parents to children to grandkids and even great grandkids.

Bowling is different things to different people. To some, it is a hard-fought competitive sport. To others, it's a relaxing form of recreation. To even more people, it's a great way to raise money for charity.

Toddlers and other youngsters may be introduced through a birthday party or their parents. Teenagers find the bowling center (or, the "bowling alley" to some people) a great place for that first date or to hang out with their friends. Husbands and wives use their biweekly or monthly league sessions as opportunities to spend quality time together. Men and women view their weekly leagues as time to hang out with the "boys" or the "girls" while fueling a strong need to compete.

You don't have to be tall, large, or fast to enjoy and succeed at bowling. Your age or physical or mental challenges and limits don't matter. While not everyone can master it, anyone can enjoy it.

Bowling wasn't always played indoors like it is today. In fact, until the late 1800s, bowling was strictly an outdoor game. Then, wealthy families who thought bowling was upscale had lanes constructed in their mansions. Later, independent establishments brought the game inside for the masses.

As an indoor activity, it no longer was subject to Mother Nature's whims. In fact, outdoor conditions often helped drive people to the sport, seeing bowling as a way to escape winter's blustery cold or summer's unbearable heat.

Today, bowling is done by families and friends, coworkers, and religious groups. It builds friendship and camaraderie while being fun. And it can bring out the competitive juices in us all.

Opposite: Bowling is becoming an extremely popular sport among high school students.

Right: In bowling, competitors make their shots by themselves, without assistance from other players.

Far right: Children of all ages enjoy the fun and competition of bowling.

Below: Competing for their country is one of the biggest honors in bowling.

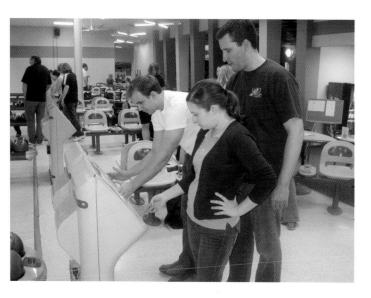

Some partake in bowling strictly for recreation rather than for competition.

There are four general ways to play the game and sport of bowling: open, league, tournament, and elite.

By far the most popular version of bowling in America is "open play." This consists of a variety of unorganized or organized options where people go to the bowling center on their own.

Unorganized open play can be friends rolling a couple of games on the spur of the moment. It can be when kids go with their parents for the first time or when a couple goes bowling on a date. It also can be when someone simply wants to practice either alone, with a coach, or with others.

Organized open play features activities such as birthday parties, religious or company outings, "glow bowling," or "rock 'n' roll bowling."

League bowling has been the backbone of the sport since the American Bowling Congress started in 1895. People form groups, called "teams," of up to five and compete on a regular basis (weekly, biweekly, monthly) for a specific period of time (weeks, months, years). Leagues set some form of competitive schedule where champions are crowned at the end of the season. Most of these groups come under the auspices of the United States Bowling Congress, which offers bowlers a variety of services to make their leagues fun and easy to run.

Tournaments are more organized activities where competition is at its fiercest. These events can take place over a day, a weekend, a month, or even several months. They range from in-center competitions to city, state, regional, or national amateur championships, to high school and collegiate varsity tournaments, to international events where medals are given for representing a bowler's country.

For some, bowling is a night out away from spouses.

Like so many other sports, a ball is an essential equipment element for bowling.

Elite bowling is performed either by top amateurs through programs such as Team USA or in the professional ranks through the Professional Bowlers Association. Team USA offers USBC members the opportunity to represent their country in international competition. PBA provides opportunities to make money not only in competition, but also through product endorsements and guest appearances.

Scores of sports and games feature some sort of spherical or ovoid object that is thrown, passed, kicked, rolled, or otherwise projected into space. Bowling is no different in that respect. But what really separates bowling from all other sports and games is the pin.

How many pins and what type of pins vary throughout the world. The most common form, especially in the United States, is tenpins, where the object is to knock over all the pins in one shot (a strike) or two (a spare) with a ball that weighs up to 16 pounds and is 27 inches around.

New England states feature a form of bowling called candlepins with tall, narrow pins and a smaller ball. Mid-Atlantic states feature

Left: The venue where bowling takes place is called a bowling center or bowling alley, and can be mom-and-pop or corporate owned.

Below: The crashing of bowling pins unmistakably tells people what game they are playing.

duckpins with short, squat pins and a smaller ball. In Canada, five-pins is a popular form of bowling. Like any game or sport, bowling has its own unique places to play. They're called bowling centers, and without them, there would be no bowling.

Bowling centers in the United States have ranged from two to 106 lanes. They exist in a variety of settings, from basements of taverns to sections of large shopping complexes to facilities attached to hotels and casinos. They are located in small towns and large, in central cities, and in growing suburbs.

No matter what the differences in size, location, or style, all certified bowling centers feature lanes the same length and width and pins the same shape. Such equipment is certified by the United States Bowling Congress each year as a service to its members. Few other sports go to such lengths to ensure its playing fields are the same from Maine to California, from Washington to Florida, and from Puerto Rico to U.S. military bases worldwide.

Whether played at a birthday party, as part of a first date, as a way for husbands and wives to spend quality time together, or in competition where trophies or money are won, bowling is something people usually think about with fondness.

Bowling centers in the United States range from two lanes to more than a hundred.

Although the game is not native to the United States, for nearly two centuries, bowling has been part of mainstream America. The route it took to get there is part of the lore of the much-loved game of bowling, America's great indoor pastime.

ANCIENT BEGINNINGS
AND EUROPEAN ROOTS

SO EXACTLY WHEN did bowling begin? Actually, nobody knows for sure. It is widely believed that Stone Age people rolled or threw round-shaped rocks and stones at other, more slender stones set up in some type of formation. This was consistent with what seems to be an innate human urge to roll or throw things at other things.

Cavemen and -women were thought to have originated a game called "duck-on-the-rocks" during which players would throw stones to try to knock a large stone off another large stone or tree stump. If this is considered

People of the Stone Age are believed to have played a primitive version of bowling using rocks and stones.

The earliest documented sign of bowling was in ancient Egypt, where stone balls were rolled at stone pins.

some ancient version of bowling, the game may indeed have started millions of years ago.

What is documented as the first official sign of bowling was in Egypt. An expedition by noted British Egyptologist Sir William Matthew Flinders Petrie in 1932 uncovered artifacts in a young boy's grave at a site called el-Gerza. Although primitive, the nine pieces of stone at which a stone ball seemed to have been rolled through a marble archway were much more consistent with the modern tenpin game than anything before it.

Dating methods at that time estimated the find to be from about 5200 B.C. More sophisticated techniques such as Carbon-14 chemical analysis prompted archaeologists and anthropologists in the early 1990s to change the dating to 3200 B.C. A second expedition in 2002 uncovered a primitive bowling alley estimated to be 1,700 years old.

In addition, ancient Polynesians on the South Sea Islands played a game called "ula maike" during which they rolled polished stones on paths at other stones 60 feet away—the same distance from the foul line to the headpin in today's bowling game.

So whether millions or thousands of years old, it would be hard to find a game older than bowling.

Exactly how and when bowling moved from Egypt remains a mystery. It could have been through Greeks before the millennium or second-century Roman legionnaires.

Ancient Polynesians played a game called "ula maike" on their South Pacific islands.

Sometime more than two thousand years ago, an underhand tossing of stones at others was thought to have been done in the Italian Alps. This likely was the start of *bocce* or lawn bowling, a game still enjoyed today, especially by those of Italian descent.

Another game called *Basque Quilles* began to spring up in Europe. It used a wooden ball likely made of tree roots and featured a slot-like grip. Players held the balls while swinging toward 3-foot-tall pins arranged in a rectangle of three rows of three pins each. The goal was to hit pins that would knock into others in a domino effect.

German bowler and historian William Pehle wrote that around the third century A.D., bowling took place in his country not as a game but as part of a religious ritual to assure salvation. While the village priest watched, parishioners would roll a rounded stone at a pin known as the *heide*, which represented the devil. If the heide fell, all sins were erased. Pity must have been taken on those who failed in this effort, and fortunately this rite lasted only about two hundred years, a blip in the arc of history.

Even the famous theologian Martin Luther began playing it after 1500 A.D. to help blow off steam. He enjoyed it enough that he had a lane built for his children and determined that nine would be the ideal number of pins. That helped standardize the game because versions of bowling began to spring up featuring as few as three pins and as many as seventeen.

Once bowling became more accepted by religious communities, it began moving more toward a sport. It also began moving from playing with objects made of stone to those made of wood. For example, early pins often were made of animal bones and later of fruitwoods.

Famous theologian
Martin Luther
bowled to blow
off steam.

Early bowling lanes, like these in Europe, all were outdoors.

With bowling becoming more accepted, it became a game to be played by rich and poor alike. It also began taking on different variations throughout Europe and Scandinavia. Most variations were developed in England, Germany, and France including:

- *Kegelspiele*, a form of German ninepins.
- *Quilles de Neuf*, a French version featuring 3-foot-tall pins on a square.
- Lawn bowling, an English game that King Edward III (1312–77) outlawed for a time so troops could instead concentrate on archery practice.
- *Bocce*, an Italian version without pins started in the 1300s, kind of like curling on grass.
- Skittles, an English version of ninepins in which fifth-century tribes used sheep bones to knock pins down. Tenpins, candlepins, and duckpins all descended from this game.
- Bowls, an English version similar to bocce often referenced by writer William Shakespeare.
- Four Corners, an English large ball game with four pins set in a square.
- *Quatre Coins*, a French game where players throw a wooden disk that resembled a wheel of cheese at several pins in four corners.
- *Pétanque*, a French version related to bocce and still popular today where a metallic ball is rolled or tossed at a small wooden target.
- *Les Quilles*, a French ninepin game in which the pins are arranged in a square and the ball can't leave the square while hitting two or more pins.
- Bomble Puppy, an English variation with a large flat area where numbered holes are dug out on one end and a ball is rolled at the highest numbered hole.
- Tether ball, an English ninepin game where a tethered ball knocks down pins.

Bowling's European roots also helped define some of the lingo still known today. For example, the word "kegler" came from the German word *kegel*, which means "bowl." The word "alley," which described the game's playing surface, came from the French word *aller*, meaning "to go."

Early alleys, or lanes as they are more modernly called, most often were made of hand-packed dirt, cinders, or clay, treated specially and baked in the sun to resemble concrete. By the thirteenth century, lanes were made of wooden planks and later covered or moved into sheds. This gave people the idea to move the game indoors, which first happened in London in 1455. For the first time, bowling could be considered a year-round activity not affected by Mother Nature.

Pehle's research also discovered bowling's ties to food, drink, and gambling as early as 1325. Interestingly, alcohol and gambling prompted government officials in England to attempt to end bowling as a sport. In 1511, England's King Henry VIII tried to ban bowling by deeming it evil because it was played in saloons where excess gambling took place. The ban officially lasted until 1845, but unofficially it was rarely observed since most of Henry's successors enjoyed the game. In contrast, Scotland thought so much of bowling that it deemed it the national sport in the sixteenth century. The Scots later worked on standardizing rules and play.

European lanes usually were constructed of dirt, cinder, or clay. Later lanes consisted of wooden planks that were covered or put in sheds.

Even though England's King Henry VIII tried to ban bowling, many of his subjects played the game anyway.

The first indication of bowling in the United States occurred in the early 1600s, when Dutch settlers brought their version of lawn bowling to New York City's Battery Park on what is still known as Bowling Green.

Although it is unknown exactly when bowling at pins first came to the United States, lawn bowling moved across the Atlantic Ocean as early as 1623, when British settlers brought lawn bowls to Manhattan Island. One of the first playing areas was at the tip of the island in Battery Park, a place still known as Bowling Green.

Dutch explorers under Henry Hudson, an English explorer and navigator, may have brought an outdoor version of skittles to the new world in the 1650s. What is known is that the earliest known reference to bowling at pins in America was made by author Washington Irving in the following passage of *Rip Van Winkle* in 1818:

On entering the amphitheater, new objects of wonder presented themselves. On a level spot in the centre was a company of odd-looking personages playing at ninepins ... Nothing interrupted the stillness of the scene but the noise of the balls, which, whenever they were rolled, echoed along the mountains like rumbling peals of thunder ...

The ensuing mass migration of Europeans to the United States would only serve to increase bowling's popularity throughout the remainder of the nineteenth century.

Left: The earliest known literary reference to bowling at pins in America was made by author Washington Irving in *Rip Van Winkle*.

Below: Dutch settlers continued to play bowling in America well into and beyond the 1650s.

COMING TO AMERICA

A T THE START of the nineteenth century, only 5.3 million people were living in a United States that was less than twenty-five years old. By the start of the twentieth century, that number had multiplied to more than 79 million.

Part of that growth came from the addition of twenty-nine states into the Union. But another major reason was the arrival of 25 million people from Western Europe, many of whom came to escape political and religious turmoil in their homelands.

Some of those immigrants were skilled craftsmen. Others were unskilled, but nearly all found work in the growing industrial centers of their new country. Many brought with them their love of bowling, including the many versions of the outdoor game played in their native countries.

Ninepins was among the most popular overseas, and it was the most frequently played version in the United States early in the century. A group of German settlers even took their ninepin game all the way to Texas, where it is still played in towns near San Antonio.

Historians believe that bowling at ten pins began in the 1820s in New York City, and by the 1830s, bowling at pins spread across the country. So too did bowling's attachment to gambling, which some people and government officials detested. The state of Connecticut even went so far as to prohibit the ninepin game in 1841, and the ban spread elsewhere in New England and threatened New York. Some time after that, however, the tenth pin was added, and whether it was done to circumvent the laws or not, it became the standard game and helped fuel its popularity.

Also helping increase bowling's allure was the opening of the Knickerbocker Alleys in New York City in 1840. The first indoor lanes, made of baked clay and located in the facility's basement, allowed people to compete at any time regardless of the weather. Ensuing years saw indoor facilities built in cities with large German populations, including Milwaukee, Wisconsin; Syracuse, New York; Cincinnati, Ohio; Buffalo, New York; and Chicago.

Opposite:
As bowling moved indoors in the latter half of the 1800s, more women became part of the sport.

Bowling in the 1870s in places like Baltimore, Maryland, primarily was conducted as an all-men's activity.

During the nineteenth century, many millions of people came to America, primarily from Europe. They brought with them their love of bowling.

Moving indoors also brought women into the sport through their own clubs. Until then, however, bowling had been almost exclusively a men's sport, where members would enjoy the game, partake in tournaments among

members, and occasionally challenge other clubs to matches.

The introduction of women helped bring bowling more respectability. Women literally helped clean up the game by helping to eliminate spittoons, cursing, filthy conditions, and unshaven men. A group of women in Lincoln, Illinois, even took matters into their own hands by destroying liquor and tobacco supplies at Boyd's Bowling Saloon.

By the 1850s, bowling received so much respect that it began to be considered an appropriate activity for upscale business leaders. Among the famous wealthy families building lanes in their mansions were the Jay Goulds in Tarrytown, New York, and Lakewood, New Jersey; George Vanderbilt's Biltmore estate in Asheville, North Carolina; the Harrimans in Newburgh, New York; the R. J. Reynolds mansion in Greenwich, Connecticut; and the fifty-two-room mansion of salt tycoon J. Sterling Morton in Nebraska City, Nebraska.

While bowling was gaining respectability and spreading to cities across the country, there was no national organization to standardize playing rules and equipment specifications. Because of the different versions brought over

During the late 1800s and early 1900s, women bowled in the long dresses that were in fashion.

Women brought respectability to bowling by helping to clean up the game and its reputation.

from Europe, the size and weight of the bowling balls, pins, and lanes varied from club to club and alley to alley. Some clubs allowed three deliveries per frame, others two. In some places a perfect score was 200; in others, it was 300. Even the definition of "amateur bowler" differed.

The first attempt to standardize the game occurred when twenty-seven delegates from nine mostly German-American New York-area bowling clubs met in 1875 to organize the National Bowling Association. Although some of the rules and specifications set then still remain today, the organization itself lasted just a few years. Another short-lived attempt occurred with the formation of the American Amateur Union in 1890. Just a few years earlier, in 1885, the United Bowling Clubs of New York formed, and it lasted many years

After numerous attempts to standardize the game, it finally came to pass in 1895 at Beethoven Hall in New York City with the formation of the American Bowling Congress.

But it primarily concentrated its efforts locally, focusing on providing members opportunities to meet on the alleys for competition, good fellowship, and entertainment.

Finally, after years of continuous disagreement, a small group of men from several cities gathered at Beethoven Hall near New York's Greenwich Village and reached an agreement during a fifteen-hour meeting on September 9, 1895. The American Bowling Congress was born.

Soon after, copies of the new agreement were mailed to bowling groups in the United States and Canada. Within a few months, there were members in Buffalo, Cincinnati, Boston, Chicago, St. Louis, Kansas City, Lowell, Massachusetts, and Wheeling, West Virginia, and even in Quebec.

This beginning of organized bowling featured playing rules for fair, ethical play and standardized equipment specifications. Much of what was established that day remains in effect throughout the world today, including 300 as maximum score and 12 inches between pins.

Among the driving forces in that initial meeting were Thomas Curtis, Dr. Henry Timm, Sam Karpf, and Joe Thum. Curtis, who was credited with writing bowling's first set of rules in 1875, was the new organization's first president. Timm was the ABC's second president, after playing a major role in establishing the organization's acceptance and stability. Karpf was the group's first secretary (he later moved the organization's headquarters to Dayton, Ohio). While one of the ABC's driving forces, Thum became known more as the father of international bowling.

With the establishment of rules and standards, bowling could now concentrate on increasing participation rather than on arguing over rules and equipment. The next major growth phase happened in 1896 when Thum, a bowling alley owner since 1881, brought bowling out of the basement with above-ground lanes at his White Elephant Saloon in New York.

Bowling was going mainstream. What had flourished in Europe before the 1800s had become fully assimilated into an American culture ready to head into the twentieth century.

Above, left to right:

Thomas Curtis was known as the "Father of Bowling" and was elected the ABC's first president.

The ABC's first secretary, Samuel Karpf added credibility and direction to the position.

Joseph Thum was considered the "father of international bowling."

The ABC's founding father, Dr. Henry Timm, served as the organization's second president.

BOWLING BECOMES ALL-INCLUSIVE

WHILE THE CREATION of the American Bowling Congress gave the sport some stability by standardizing rules and equipment and setting the stage for its eventual growth, it still reflected the nation's views of women and minorities as the twentieth century began.

In a country that didn't allow women to vote until 1920, bowling remained a game played primarily by white men in saloon alleys. Although women's participation increased in the late 1800s and there was evidence of women participating in leagues as far back as 1892, it still wasn't seen as a lady-like activity.

To avoid ruining their reputations, many women had to sneak into the alleys—with or without their husbands. Some bowled behind partitions or drapes or only when men were not present. Those who did bowl did so in fancy yet uncomfortable clothing such as high-button shoes and ankle-length skirts.

Efforts to compete with the men initially proved fruitless. When the ABC held its first nationwide tournament in 1901, the forty-one teams from nine states competing over four days on lanes in Chicago's Welsbach Building were all made of white men. Women were only allowed their own small separate tournament at Chicago's Mussey's Alleys.

In 1904, a center in Dayton, Ohio, opened lanes on the second floor only for women bowlers. Women finally were allowed on the same ABC tournament lanes as the men in 1907, but only after the conclusion of the St. Louis event.

Still, that competition was significant as seven top Midwest bowlers plus twelve teams competed to determine the nation's best women bowlers. A team from Doe Run, Missouri, captured the team title while St. Louis star Berdie Kern, who claimed to be the world's best female bowler, won the singles title with a 543 score for three games.

Among the men most proud of that feat was St. Louis bowling center owner and sports writer Dennis Sweeney, who organized the women's event after starting a women's league at his establishment. He was an advocate of

Opposite:
Women of the 1950s and 1960s showed off a keen sense of fashion on the bowling lanes.

Bowling for women began growing in the late 1800s and early 1900s.

women becoming ABC members as he felt bowling would never become a major sport until it was accepted by women. He hoped the St. Louis tournament would persuade others to agree with him.

When Sweeney's efforts failed, avid bowler Ellen Kelly formed the St. Louis Women's Bowling Association in 1915. Using contacts provided by Sweeney, she wrote to other bowling proprietors seeking bowlers to form a national women's organization.

With Sweeney's help, Kelly conducted the first true women's national championships with titles decided in team, doubles, singles, and all-events (the total scores of team, doubles, and singles) divisions. After the tournament, Sweeney, Kelly, and fellow bowlers Cornelia Berghaus and Catherine Menne gathered forty women from eleven cities at Sweeney's Washington Recreation Parlor on November 28, 1916, and formed the Women's National Bowling Association. Later, members from Canada and Mexico were added and the name was changed

Since its beginnings in 1916, the WIBC Tournament has attracted women from around the country who showed off both their on-lanes skills and their fashion sense.

Left: While many were fighting in World War II, teams like South St. Louis Dairy were holding things together back home.

Below: While women often had to sneak their way into bowling alleys in the late 1800s and early 1900s, thanks to the formation of the Women's International Bowling Congress in 1916, teams of women from all over the country participated in leagues and tournaments at the local, state, and national levels.

27

WIBC raised enough money to donate an airplane called Miss Nightingale II to the U.S. World War II effort.

Eric deFreitas helped form numerous junior leagues and tournaments and guided many young black bowlers into better competitions and the pros.

to the Women's International Bowling Congress, which lasted until 2004. (In 2005, the WIBC merged with the ABC, the Young American Bowling Alliance, and USA Bowling to form the United States Bowling Congress.)

WIBC eventually grew into the world's largest and most successful women's sports organization with as many as 4 million members. For nearly eighty years, it was the only bowling organization for women.

Now bowling could truly come out of its basement saloon atmosphere and become an activity respectable enough for women to enjoy. The trouble was that not all men and women were allowed to enjoy it equally. Just as the nation itself was slow to acknowledge social and economic change, so, too, was bowling.

Although few people of color took part in bowling early in the 1900s, ABC and WIBC made it even harder to do so by adopting rules in 1916 and 1921, respectively, limiting their memberships to white males and white females. Society being what it was then, such legislation barely caused a ripple.

Like the women years before them, African-American bowlers had to rent lanes for after-hours private parties or sneak into the back entrance to avoid white patrons or ABC backlash against proprietors who allowed them into their establishments.

The first time nonwhites were allowed into organized bowling was in the mid-1930s when people of Asian descent were moving into Hawaii. Thanks to the efforts of Honolulu bowling alley owner J. J. Kelly, membership eligibility rules were amended in 1936 to allow nonwhites in outlying U.S. possessions to become full ABC members.

Because this created a new inequality where nonwhites outside the continental United States had rights those within it did not, the rule was modified again in 1942. This time, city associations in outlying possessions or foreign countries were allowed to accept nonwhite members but only for local leagues and tournaments. Nonwhites still could not join the ABC or the WIBC, and they could not participate in their national tournaments.

Sydney Celestine helped lead the fight to force ABC to eliminate its Caucasian-only rule in 1950.

Meanwhile, African-American participation was growing to a point that allowed for the first separate national tournament, held in Cleveland in May 1939. Three months later, the Negro National Bowling Association was formed in Detroit. The name was changed in 1944 to The National Bowling Association, and the group remains strong today with members of all genders and races.

In 1941, J. Elmer Reed and two partners built the first African-American-owned bowling center in Cleveland. Four years later, the first African-American league was formed by Eric deFreitas in Brooklyn. By 1947, an article in *Ebony* magazine said bowling was the most popular sport among African Americans, with an average of 15,000 playing nightly.

Rokuro "Fuzzy" Shimada was instrumental in promoting bowling to Japanese Americans who, until 1950, could not belong to the American Bowling Congress.

Such growing participation spurred talks with the ABC and the WIBC to end their years of discrimination. The National Bowling Association, the Japanese American Citizens League, B'nai B'rith, Catholic Youth Organization, United Auto Workers– Congress of Industrial Organizations, and the National Committee for Fair Play in Bowling all expressed the belief that bowling should be desegregated. Key individuals like deFreitas, Reed, TNBA President Sydney Celestine, boxer Joe Louis, Reverend Charles Carow, labor leader Walter Reuther, and U.S. Senators James Mead and Hubert Humphrey reinforced the concern about discrimination in bowling.

The ABC and the WIBC had argued that as membership organizations, they had the right to determine their own members. But with younger, more liberal people like Frank Baker leading the

ABC and the threat of several lawsuits—as well as the fear of losing in the court of public opinion—the ABC and the WIBC finally eliminated "white" from their membership rules in 1950. The end of this unfortunate era in bowling history was best illustrated when Detroit's Allen Supermarket became the first black team at the 1951 ABC Tournament.

Despite the struggles of the era, one bright spot emerged with the beginnings of organized youth bowling. What started with one Chicago intramural league in 1936 blossomed into a citywide program of more than 8,000 participants. By 1945, the old National Bowling Council provided financial support to take the program national, and in 1946, the American Junior Bowling Congress was formed.

J. Elmer Reed was the first black member of the ABC Hall of Fame.

Left: Bowling became even more popular after restrictions on minority membership were lifted.

Bottom left: Detroit's Allen Supermarket was the first all-black team to compete in the American Bowling Congress Championships Tournament in 1951 after the repeal in 1950 of the ABC's whites-only membership rule.

The AJBC merged with two other groups to form the Young American Bowling Alliance in 1982. The ABC and the WIBC remained separate organizations for men and women until the threat of more lawsuits prompted the ABC to remove "male" from its constitution in 1994. The YABA and the WIBC remained all-youth and all-women's organizations until 2005, when they merged with the ABC and USA Bowling to form the United States Bowling Congress.

Bottom right: Chicago's Milt Raymer formed the American Junior Bowling Congress to welcome youth into the game.

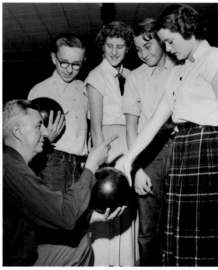

BOWLING GOES MODERN

N THE FIRST HALF of the twentieth century, while the sport was determining where and with whom people could compete, bowling also enjoyed a visual and mechanical modernization period like no other.

By the end of the 1950s, the very look and feel of where people bowled would change dramatically—all intended to create a cleaner, family-friendly atmosphere that would help attract new audiences. The interiors and exteriors of the bowling alleys were vastly upgraded while electronic inventions helped automate the game.

Among the changes were the development of streamlined lanes, colorful semicircle leatherette seats, and screens that hid human pinsetters called "pinboys" from view. There also was the creation of the electronic foul detector and Tel-E-Score overhead projector.

But no technological advance to bowling before or since was larger than the introduction of the automatic pinsetters in the late 1940s. Affectionately called mechanical pinboys, they replaced the young people who had manually set pins since the late nineteenth century.

Pinboys had two main tasks: They cleared and reset appropriate pins by hand-loading them into a pinsetter and pushing the rack down to reset the pins, and they placed the bowling balls on the return ramp to roll back to the bowlers after each shot. Later, semi-automatic devices allowed the pinboys to set the pins in a rack and then pull a string that lowered the pins into the deck.

Being a pinboy was a thankless, repetitive job. The pits where they sat behind and above the pins were hot, stuffy, cramped, and full of smoke from the cigars and cigarettes many of their patrons smoked. Pinboys suffered plenty of bruised knees and shins from the pins flying around the pits.

During World War II, bowling centers were unable to find enough reliable pinboys to work, so the development of the automatic pinsetter was a welcome solution that also helped speed up and clean up the game.

Development of the automatic pinsetter actually was years in the making. Bowling alley owner George Beckerle of Pearl River, New York, had the

Opposite:
Modernized
bowling centers
helped create a
cleaner, brighter
atmosphere
that attracted
new players.

Being a pinboy wasn't at all glamorous as there were plenty of injuries to go around.

Pinboys were a big part of bowling's lore from the late 1800s until the middle 1900s, when they were replaced by automatic pinsetters.

initial idea in the early 1930s. One of his customers, Gottfried Schmidt, w intrigued enough to recruit friends John McElroy and Fred Sandhage to he build a prototype in the turkey house on Sandhage's farm. Using lampshad

nd flower pots, they created a suction system they believed could eliminate what was perceived as the bondage of the pinboys.

They pitched their model to officials at the Brunswick Corporation but vere turned down because of its perceived high cost. But one Brunswick mployee, Robert Kennedy, thought differently and when he moved to rival AMF, he brought it to the attention of his new boss, Morehead Patterson.

The introduction of semi-automatic pinsetters gave some relief to pinboys.

Semi-automatic pinsetters allowed pinboys to set pins in a rack and push down on the rack to set the pins.

35

Patterson agreed with the concept and after much refinement to cut costs and improve efficiency, AMF bought the patent in 1946 and displayed samples at that year's American Bowling Congress Tournament in Buffalo, New York. The process would have occurred several years earlier had it not been for World War II. Five years later, the AMF A-1 was approved by the

Pinboys in action loading semi-automatic pinsetters.

ABC for commercial installation. AMF had the market to itself until 1956, when Brunswick introduced its B-1 automatic pinspotter spearheaded by Vice President Milt Rudo.

Rudo also came up with several other concepts at Brunswick to improve the game. In the early 1950s, he recommended taking chalk and hand towels out of the approach area to speed up the game. He also broadened national use of the Tel-E-Score overhead score projector and worked to have the industry accept synthetic rubber balls and gain acceptance of the laminated bowling pin.

The Tel-E-Score was invented by John Coker, an electronics whiz who installed Alexander Graham Bell's first personal telephone. It allowed bowlers and fans to easily see their scores on screens over the lane approaches rather than looking over scorekeepers' shoulders.

Coker, an early Western movie actor who later became a San Diego bowling alley owner, also invented the electronic foul detector in 1937 to replace human foul judges and keep people from ruining lane finishes by sliding past the foul line in their street shoes. It was approved for use by the ABC in 1951.

Modern automatic pinsetters put pinboys out of work by the early 1950s.

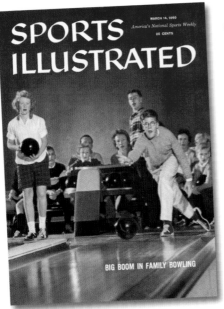

Sports Illustrated touted the growing popularity of bowling in its November 14, 1960, issue, one of the rare covers to feature the game.

Another innovation during this time was the invention of the plastic-coated bowling pin by Omaha, Nebraska, businessman Henry Moore and his wife Margaret. Designed to double the life of the previously all-wood bowling pins, the Moores started their journey in 1947, and after extensive testing, the ABC approved them in 1954.

The 1940s and '50s also proved to be an era of modern architecture. Led by the more than fifty centers designed by California architects Gordon Powers, Austin Daly, and Pat DeRosa, bowling establishments displayed a new style. They looked more space age with brightly lit and midcentury-modern design. They featured fancy outdoor signs, some with replica pins, neon lights with starbursts, or high-flying arrows.

The invention of air conditioning also benefited bowling in that people now had a place to go to in order to get out of the stifling summer heat found in the northern part of the country and the year-round heat in the emerging Sun Belt region.

The late 1960s brought another technological advance with the computerized scoring system. Originally conceived about the same time as

As bowling moved into the 1950s and 1960s, old, rundown bowling alleys were replaced by modern bowling centers.

38

he automatic pinsetter, the automatic scorer meant people no longer had o score by hand using a grease pencil to show up on the Tel-E-Scores.

Bowling's modern advances meant it could become a year-round, otentially twenty-four-hour recreation. Now all the sport needed were ways o tell the world about its modern amenities.

Clean, modern centers of the midtwentieth century included fancy signs to attract people passing by.

BOWLING MOVES INTO
THE BIG TIME

FOR THE THIRTEEN YEARS between 1920 and 1933, Prohibition directly affected bowling's long association with taverns and alcohol. The 18th Amendment of the U.S. Constitution and subsequent Volstead Act attempted to reduce the use of alcohol and alcoholism by prohibiting the sale, manufacture, and distribution of alcohol. But Prohibition did more than just close down breweries, distilleries, and vintners.

Although the federal government didn't completely enforce the rules and life continued as usual for many people, alcohol-related companies didn't sponsor bowling during that time. But that quickly changed once the 21st Amendment to repeal Prohibition was ratified in December 1933. By early 1934, famous breweries like Pabst, Hamm's, Stroh's, Meister Brau, Falstaff, and later Anheuser-Busch began sponsoring semiprofessional teams, many of which enjoyed success at major events like the American Bowling Congress Tournament.

The early beer-sponsored teams in the 1930s featured future hall of famers like Chicago's Ed Krems with Pabst; Paul Krumske with Meister Brau; Detroit's Joe Norris with the white-flannel uniformed Stroh's Bohemian Beer; Fred Bujack, Therm Gibson, Lou Sielaff, and George Young with E&B/Pfeiffer; and Basil "Buzz" Fazio with Stroh's.

The biggest era of beer team bowling, however, dawned in the 1950s as the major breweries again paid groups of players to represent them across the country. It all started in 1954 when former St. Louis police sergeant and master promoter Whitey Harris convinced Anheuser-Busch to sponsor a team. He recruited greats like Ray Bluth, Don Carter, Tom Hennessey, Pat Patterson, and Dick Weber, and their star power helped put the Budweisers and bowling in the media limelight. The team's biggest moment came the night of March 12, 1958, with a 3,878 overall series, a record that stood for thirty-six years.

Anheuser-Busch rival brewery Falstaff brought in Fazio and later another hall of famer, Tony Lindemann, from Detroit to try to match the Buds. Another Detroit-based team, the Pfeiffers, were led by Bill Lillard, who later

Opposite:
One of the sport's greatest bowlers, Don Carter was part of the famous St. Louis Budweisers during the height of the beer-team era.

In the mid-1900s, beer-sponsored teams traveled the country to battle with squads backed by other breweries.

After the repeal of Prohibition in 1933, teams sponsored by American breweries began touring the country. Legendary Joe Norris (third from right) led many of these teams.

competed with Chicago's Falstaffs. Bob Strampe led Detroit's Stroh's team. The beer era was in full swing.

Another phenomenon that took hold in the United States at this time was television. As the technology spread across the country in the late 1940s

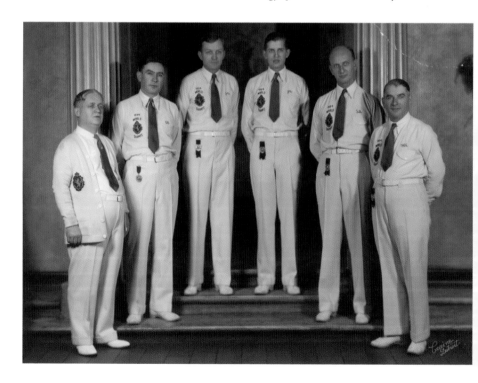

At the height of the beer team era in the 1960s, the St. Louis Budweisers were the most famous group. They included, front row, from left: Whitey Harris, Pat Patterson, and Don Carter; back row: Bill Lillard, Ray Bluth, Dick Weber, and Tom Hennessey. Many of these bowlers helped start the Professional Bowlers Association.

and early 1950s, programming to fill the airwaves became even more important. And that fit bowling perfectly.

With its small studio-like venue providing good lighting and needing few cameras, bowling was a perfect partner for this new medium. Long-running

As television grew in importance, so too did bowling thanks to shows like "Championship Bowling."

Television stars like Dick Cavett (left) and Don Adams (right) showed their love for bowling in the 1960s.

"Celebrity Bowling" featuring stars like Cesar Romero and Elizabeth Allen were popular in the 1970s.

local bowling shows quickly began airing, especially in major markets. Bringing the sport into people's homes several times a week, these live and taped shows quickly made heroes of local and national competitors and helped emphasize that bowling was for everyone.

One such program, "Chicago's Championship Bowling," originally hosted by hall of famer Joe Wilman began a fifteen-year national syndication run in 1955 and later featured legendary broadcaster Chris Schenkel.

Shows like "Celebrity Bowling" hosted by actor Jed Allan, "Make That Spare," and Milton Berle's "Jackpot Bowling" aired nationally. USBC Hall of Famer John Klares was a technical advisor and later umpire on "Jackpot Bowling." A television show concept called "Bowling for Dollars" was franchised regionally and locally.

Television's success with bowling caught the eye of Akron Ohio, attorney Eddie Elias in 1958

He saw a tremendous opportunity to promote the sport and its stars
as individuals rather than as members of famous teams. So he recruited many
of the top beer team members to help him form the Professional Bowlers
Association. Thus ended the beer team era.

Elias patterned the PBA after the Professional Golfers Association Tour
where the players were full-time competitors, not part-time pros who held
other jobs. He started with three events in 1959 and seven in 1960. Then in
1962, Elias secured a deal to broadcast the tour on the national American
Broadcasting Company network and bowling truly took off.

Every Saturday until 1998, the PBA Tour showcased the world's best
bowlers. In its early years, it helped pro bowlers become better known and
better paid than athletes in some other sports. A few earned as much as
$100,000 and many $50,000 or more when product endorsement, retainers,

The show
"Jackpot Bowling"
was broadcast
across the nation
and hosted by
comedian
Milton Berle.

The Professional Bowlers Association made stars of players like Earl Anthony every Saturday afternoon on ABC-TV for nearly four decades.

and royalty fees were included. For many years, it also pulled in more viewers than all but a few major sporting events.

PBA became a weekly ritual for millions of Americans, helping fuel the nation's passion for the sport. The telecasts helped introduce the country not only to established stars like Carter and Weber in the 1960s, but also to later standouts like Earl Anthony (the sport's first $1 million lifetime earnings winner) in the 1970s, Mike Aulby, Marshall Holman, and Mark Roth in the 1980s, and Walter Ray Williams, Jr. in the 1990s. It also made household names of broadcasters Schenkel, Billy Welu, and Nelson Burton, Jr.

With much less fanfare, the nation's top women formed their own professional organization in 1959, the Women's Professional Bowling Association. Among the founders were hall of famers Georgia Veatch, Marion Ladewig, Sylvia Wene Martin, LaVerne Carter, Shirley Garms, and Helen Duval.

Later, organizations like the Ladies Pro Bowlers Tour and Professional Women's Bowling Association helped produce stars like Betty Morris and Donna Adamek in the 1970s, Lisa Wagner and Aleta Sill in the 1980s, and Tish Johnson and Wendy Macpherson in the 1990s. While the men on the PBA Tour flourished on television, women pros had a much harder time establishing themselves on the airwaves.

Still, television and professional bowling were instrumental in bowling's astonishing growth in the United States, which in 1980 featured nearly 9 million men, women, and children participating in weekly leagues. That put American bowling well ahead of the rest of the world, even in the places where the sport originated. That's because while modern tenpin centers had become popular in the United States, they were rare even in Europe.

Interestingly, U.S. bowlers rarely faced those outside the country during the first half of the twentieth century. USBC Hall of Famer Joe Thum did bring the best U.S. bowlers to Sweden in 1923 and on other European trips in 1926 and 1929, and he hosted European teams in New York in 1934. He also led a team that competed in the 1936 special event held in conjunction with and before the Olympic Games in Berlin, Germany.

It wasn't until the United States joined the Federation Internationale des Quilleurs in the early 1960s that Americans would again compete with their international peers. FIQ was formed in the early 1950s by a group of European nations for competition with nonprofessional bowlers.

U.S. men began competing in the FIQ American Zone Championships in 1962 and first joined the women in the World Championships in 1963. American men were part of a new event called the AMF World Cup from its 1965 inception with women's competition included starting in 1972.

With professional bowling's television popularity on the rise and the sport growing internationally, the seeds for a bright future truly had been planted.

Through events like the World Championships, bowling began expanding internationally.

MODERN BOWLING TAKES
ON A DIFFERENT LOOK

While men and women have bowled in leagues since after World War II, it wasn't until 1994 they could compete together at events like the ABC/USBC Open Championships.

Bᴇᴛᴡᴇᴇɴ World War II and the end of the 1970s, bowling enjoyed growth in participation like it had never seen before. With so many technological advances introduced during that time and a big influx of women, youth, and minorities, it's no wonder.

There were just 250,000 members of the Women's International Bowling Congress in the 1945–46 season shortly after the epic global battle ended. By the early 1960s, that had increased tenfold. In the 1978–79 season, a record 4,232,000 women were competing in weekly leagues.

Inaugural membership in the American Junior Bowling Congress was 8,767 in 1946–47. That expanded to 451,000 in 1962–63 and to more than

Despite drops in league participation since 1980, youth bowlers still enjoy the competition and camaraderie of bowling and are the future of the sport.

53,000 in 1978–79. While the more established all-male American Bowling Congress didn't see the same growth rate, it grew from an estimated 810,000 at war's end to more than 4 million in 1979–80, still a period of fantastic growth. In addition to the growth in population, the number of bowling centers also increased dramatically during this period. While there were about 5,000 U.S. centers when World War II ended, there were nearly 11,000 by 1962–63.

To help more people enjoy their bowling experience, an increased emphasis on coaching has taken place in recent years.

As the country entered the 1980s, more than 9 million adults and youth were participating in primarily weekly leagues in nearly 8,700 establishments. Bowling truly was a part of the American fabric.

But then a broad series of changes in American society that remain today soon began to affect bowling in ways it could neither foresee nor change. Among them:

- Women who had chosen to stay home with their children began moving into the workforce.
- Manufacturing factories in the northern tier of the country began cutting back on employees, moving to southern states or closing entirely.
- People were working more hours and moving further away from their jobs, creating longer commutes to their places of employment.
- Early technological innovations such as cable television and video cassette recorders and, later, home and entertainment options like personal computers and the Internet flooded the market.

Coaching in small groups has helped adults improve their games.

Teaching children the proper way to bowl should go a long way in expanding the sport's future reach.

• Sports such as soccer and softball attracted youth and adults alike, especially after their appearances in the 1996 Olympic Games.
• Aging owners and the value of land and property caused many bowling centers to sell or close.

The results proved monumental:

• A dramatic decrease in daytime ladies leagues.
• Late-night bowling leagues became rare.
• People were no longer committed to structured weekly activities like bowling leagues.
• More leisure time was spent at home.
• As bowlers aged, the numbers of people watching bowling on television shrunk.
• Few younger Americans were participating in bowling as a sport.
• Only 5,000 bowling centers were available for play in 2011.

Changing American society switched bowling from a weekly league ritual to something more often done just a few times a year. During the 2011–12 season, the number of overall league bowlers dropped to below 2 million for the first time in more than sixty years. Half as many centers meant there were far fewer places to play the game.

Some bowling purists tried to blame the dramatic participation drop on the proliferation of high scores caused in part by technological advances in bowling balls, lane dressings, and lane surfaces. But surveys of those who left indicated this was not a factor.

Despite these changes, bowling still shows many positive signs. While fewer people are competing in bowling as a competition, more than 70 million Americans think enough of it as a game or recreation to participate at least once a year. That's far more than any other indoor activity.

The net amount of bowling establishments has remained steady throughout much of the 2000s as older, run-down centers are being replaced by bright, new, upscale family entertainment centers and nightclub-like bowling lounges.

Bowling's future as a sport is tied to whatever success it enjoys from its youth. New programs that mimic the success of sports like soccer, Little League baseball, and softball have been created. A clear path from youth competition all the way to pros has been outlined.

Above left: Proper release is key to a good result when the ball hits the pins.

Above right: More than 70 million people enjoy bowling every year, including nearly 2 million who participate in weekly bowling leagues.

The National Collegiate Athletic Association recognizes women's bowling as a varsity sport.

Excitement reigns supreme during collegiate bowling matches held across the country.

Bowling has been one of the fastest-growing high school sport in America since before the start of the twenty-first century. The sam goes for collegiate bowlers, whose women are recognized by th National Collegiate Athletic Association. New avenues for players t

earn scholarships for both their on- and off-lane achievements have been created.

To attract very young children, the industry created bumpers, initially inflatable balloon-like tubes and later metal rails that rise from the channels to keep kids from getting discouraged when shots went astray (known as the dreaded "gutter balls"). Also introduced was bowling as part of physical education classes in elementary and middle schools. In the mid-1990s, glow-in-the-dark bowling was invented to appeal to people in their upper teens, twenties, and thirties.

Increased emphasis on teaching and coaching bowling as a sport has helped create a growing number of well-trained experts. They are able to coach bowlers from beginners to professional stars.

There's been an influx of top young stars like Chris and Lynda Barnes, Sean Rash, Liz Johnson, Kelly Kulick, and Diandra Asbaty. And, players from Australia and Europe, such as Jason Belmonte and Osku Palermaa, have introduced the United States to a new, two-handed method for throwing the ball, which is only adding to the fun of the game.

Another effort to move bowling forward came in February 2010 with the grand opening of the International Bowling Campus in Arlington, Texas. Most of bowling's major organizations, including the Bowling Proprietors' Association of America and United States Bowling Congress,

Bowling is among the fastest-growing sports in high schools.

More than twenty states recognize high school bowling as a varsity sport with nearly every other state considering it a club sport.

The United States Bowling Congress was formed in 2005 as the national governing body of bowling as recognized by the United States Olympic Committee.

as well as the new International Bowling Museum and Hall of Fame, are now located there, right in the shadow of the homes of the Texas Rangers baseball team, the Dallas Cowboys football team, and the Six Flags Over Texas amusement park.

But bowling's best hope to earn the respect it deserves both in America and beyond may lie in its ability to get into the Summer Olympics. There have been numerous attempts to make it a medal sport, with the closest try resulting in becoming an exhibition sport in 1988 in Seoul, South Korea. The sport made various appearances at other Olympics since then, but as the 2010s arrived, the International Olympic Committee still had not been not convinced to add it to their sports. While sports like table tennis, badminton, and golf have been added, bowling is still waiting.

It will take increased media exposure and sponsorship money and expansion of youth efforts worldwide to create that opportunity. With more than 100 million people playing the game in more than 100 countries and foreign growth surging, there's hope.

Bowling is one of those rare sports that can be enjoyed for a lifetime. In the United States alone, people of all ages have regularly taken to the lanes. Whether played for personal pride, as a recreation, or a competitive sport, they know what that distinctive sound of the ball rolling on the lanes and pins crashing means.

Even though bowling originated in Egypt and moved to Europe, it has truly flourished in the United States. It's the great indoor American sport.

The ultimate venue for U.S. bowlers today is Team USA, where many of the best professionals and top amateurs share in winning gold medals. Pictured from left are Rhino Page, Bill Hoffman, Tommy Jones, Patrick Allen, Walter Ray Williams Jr., Chris Barnes, and Jeri Edwards, the former Team USA head coach.

America's best women bowlers also celebrate winning medals for their country including, from left: Shannon Pluhowsky, Stefanie Nation, Shannon O'Keefe, Liz Johnson, Kelly Kulick, and Carolyn Dorin-Ballard.

BOWLING LEXICON

A

ABC—American Bowling Congress, founded in 1895, was one of four organizations that merged to form the United States Bowling Congress (USBC) on January 1, 2005. At one time, ABC was the world's largest sports membership organization. With the Women's International Bowling Congress (WIBC), ABC was an official rules-making body of tenpin bowling in the United States, Puerto Rico, and military bases worldwide.

ABSENT—A score used in league when a bowler on the team is not there to bowl.

ACTUAL—See SCRATCH.

ALLEY—See LANE.

ANCHOR—Last player in a lineup for team competition.

APPROACH—1) Portion of the lane behind the foul line used by bowlers to build momentum to deliver the ball. 2) The movement of a bowler from stance to the delivery.

ARROWS—Targets on the lane starting about 15 feet from the foul line.

ASSOCIATIONS—Name applied to volunteer organizations serving at the local and state levels for the USBC.

AVERAGE—For a bowler, the total number of pins knocked down divided by the number of games bowled.

B

BACK END—The last 15 feet of the lane before the pins.

BACK UP—See REVERSE HOOK.

BALL—The round object weighing up to 16 pounds and with a circumference of up to 27 inches that is rolled at the pins to knock them down.

BALL RACK—Storage structure where establishments keep house balls.

BALL RETURN—1) The machine that returns the ball to the player

2) Where the ball rests on or near the approach.

BALL TRACK—1) The portion of the ball that comes in contact with the lane surface. 2) The area on the lane where the majority of balls are rolled creating a worn path.

BOARD—Wooden lanes have boards approximately one inch wide. Synthetic lanes feature the same image. Bowlers use specific boards to line up their stance and as their target on various shots.

BONUS—Extra pins or points awarded during match-play competition for winning a particular match.

BOWLER'S AREA (also SETTEE)—The area where players wait between shots. Usually contains seats and a scoring unit.

BOWLING CENTER (also BOWLING ALLEY) – A facility where people go to bowl.

BROOKLYN (also CROSSOVER)—Describes a strike ball that goes to the opposite side it was intended. For example, a right-hander hitting the left side of the head pin. (In Brooklyn, it is called a "Jersey.")

C

CERTIFICATION—1) Competition registered with and conducted in accordance with USBC rules. All certified bowling centers must have their lanes inspected annually by USBC to ensure they meet specifications. 2) The accreditation earned by USBC coaches upon completion of training courses.

CHANNEL (also GUTTER)—The 10-inch out-of-bounds area to the right and left of the lane that guides the ball to the pit once it leaves the playing area.

CLEAN GAME—A game with a spare or strike in each frame.

CONCOURSE—The main walkway and spectator area in a bowling center where food and drinks should be kept.

CONDITIONER—See LANE CONDITIONER.

CONTROL DESK—The main hub in a bowling center where all lane activity is managed.

CONVENTIONAL GRIP—The grip in which the fingers are inserted up to the second knuckle and the thumb is fully inserted; recommended for beginning bowlers.

COUNT—Number of pins knocked down on each ball.

CRANKER—A bowling style that describes a bowler who throws a powerful hook.

CROSSOVER—See BROOKLYN.

CUSHION—The padding at the rear of the pit to absorb the shock of the ball and pins.

D

DEAD BALL (also FLAT BALL)—1) An ineffective ball that deflects badly when it hits the pins. 2) Can be declared at delivery if any of a variety of factors occurs as listed in the USBC rule book. 3) Any ball that enters the channel.

DEADWOOD—Pins that fall over but remain on the lane or in the channel that must be removed before the next shot.

DELIVERY—The combination of a bowler's approach and release.

DOTS—1) Imbedded markings in the lane just past the foul line and used by some bowlers as their target. 2) A series of markings on the approach used to assist the bowler in lining up.

DOUBLE—Two consecutive strikes.

DRY LANE—A lane that has a little amount of conditioner (oil).

F

FILL—Pins knocked down following a spare or two consecutive strikes in the tenth frame.

FINGERTIP GRIP—The grip in which the fingers are inserted to the first knuckle and thumb fully inserted; recommended for experienced bowlers.

FLAT BALL—See DEAD BALL.

FOUL—Going beyond the foul line at delivery. Results in a zero scored for that delivery.

FOUL LINE—A solid black stripe that separates the approach from the lane.

FOUNDATION FRAME—The ninth frame. The desire is to roll a strike or spare as a "foundation" for the tenth frame.

FRAME—Each game is divided into ten frames, the first nine allowing a maximum of two shots with three shots allowed in the tenth frame.

FRONTS (also HEADS)—The first 15 feet of the lane beyond the foul line.

FULL ROLLER—A ball that rolls over its full circumference and produces a track between the thumb and fingers.

G

GRIP—The way the hand fits in the ball, either conventional or fingertip.

GUTTER—See CHANNEL.

H

HANDICAP—Pins given to individuals or teams in an attempt to equalize the competition.

HEAD PIN—The 1-pin.

HEADS—See FRONTS.

HOOK—1) A ball path that usually curves sharply near the pins. 2) The second phase of ball motion.

HOUSE—A term for a bowling center.

HOUSE BALL—Bowling ball provided by the center.

HOUSE SHOES—Rental shoes provided by the center.

HOUSE SHOT (also HOUSE CONDITION)—The oil pattern typically used by bowling centers for leagues and other events.

J

JUNIOR TEAM USA—The official USBC team comprised of male and female bowlers age twenty and younger who represent the United States in international competition.

K

KEGLER—German word for bowler. The term was used to describe bowlers for many years.

KEY PIN—In spare shooting, it is the pin that the ball must hit initially to convert a spare.

KICKBACK—Vertical division boards between lanes in the pit. On most hits, the pins bounce off the kickbacks to knock down additional pins.

Bowling moved out of the basement in 1896 when Joe Thum built his famous White Elephant Lanes in New York City above ground.

L

LANE (also ALLEY)—Playing surface made of either maple and pine wood or a synthetic surface.

LANE CONDITIONER (also LANE OIL or LANE DRESSING)—An oil used to coat or dress the lanes, necessary to protect the lane surface. Also affects the reaction of a bowling ball.

LANE FINISH—A urethane-based product placed on wood lanes to protect the lanes' surface.

LEADOFF—First player in a team lineup.

LEAGUE—A competition in which bowlers or teams of bowlers compete against others in a series of weeks or sessions.

LINE—1) The path a bowling ball takes from release to the pins. 2) One game of bowling.

LOCATOR DOTS—1) Markings imbedded in the lane

just past the foul line and used by some bowlers as their target. 2) A series of markings on the approach used to assist the bowler in lining up on the approach.

LOFT—The distance beyond the foul line that the ball travels after leaving the bowler's hand to the point of impact on the lane surface.

M

MARK—1) Getting a strike or spare in a frame. 2) The spot on the lane bowlers use as their target.

MID-LANE (also PINES)—The 30-foot section between the fronts and back end.

MISS—See OPEN.

MIXED LEAGUES—Leagues of men and women competing together.

N

NO TAP—A form of competition that awards a strike when nine pins are knocked down on the first ball. It also can be when eight pins are knocked down.

O

OIL—See LANE CONDITIONER.

OILY (also SLICK)—Indicates that there is a heavy coating of conditioner on the lane, making it difficult to hook the ball.

OPEN (also MISS)—A frame that doesn't include a strike or spare.

OPEN BOWLING—Nonleague, nontournament play; practice.

P

PARTICLE BALLS—Developed in the mid-1990s, bowling balls made using high-tech manufacturing processes to insert minute pieces of silica such as glass beads in the ball's shell to increase hook potential.

PERFECT GAME—Rolling twelve consecutive strikes in one game for a score of 300.

PIN DECK—The area at the end of the lane where the pins are set.

PINES—See MID-LANE.

PINFALL—The total count of pins knocked over in a given shot, series of shots, or games.

PINS—The free-standing targets at the end of the lane. They are set in groups of ten for each frame.

PIT—The open area behind the pin deck where pins and balls go after leaving the back of the pin deck.

PLASTIC BALLS—Developed during the 1950s and made of polyester.

POCKET (also HOLE)—Where a ball hits solidly between the 1-pin and 3-pin for right-handers and the 1-pin and 2-pin for left-handers.

POLISH—A compound used to shine bowling balls to decrease hook potential.

POT GAME—Competition in which two or more bowlers post some sort of stake on a winner-take-all basis or to be divided by the number of entrants.

R

REACTIVE RESIN BALLS—Developed in the 1990s, made of an advanced urethane. Reactive resin bowling balls increase hook potential.

RELEASE—The point at which a bowler lets go of the ball.

RELEASE POINT—The moment the bowler releases the ball with the thumb, rolling off the fingers and imparting rotation to the ball.

RESURFACE—This term refers to wood lanes, when a center cuts the worn-out, damaged lanes down to bare wood in preparation for recoating the lane finish.

REVERSE HOOK (also BACKUP)—A ball that hooks toward the hand from which the bowler delivered it. For example, a right-hander who hooks the ball to the right.

REVOLUTIONS—Also known as "revs." The amount of rotation a bowler imparts to a bowling ball as it travels from the foul line to the pins.

S

SANDBAGGER—A bowler who purposely keeps his or her average down to receive a higher handicap.

SANDING—A process used on bowling balls to increase hook potential.

SCRATCH (also ACTUAL)—A bowling score that does not include any handicap.

SEMIROLLER—A ball that rolls off its center and produces a track outside of the thumb and fingers.

SET—1) When a ball holds its line into the pocket. 2) A series of games.

SETTEE—See BOWLER'S AREA.

SHOT—1) A single delivery. 2) Reference to where to play specific types of oil patterns.

SKID—The first phase of ball motion when the ball slides though the front portion of the lane.

SLICK—See OILY.

SNOWPLOW—A ball that hits straight on the head pin and clears the pin for a strike.

SPAN—The distance between the thumb and finger holes on a bowling ball

SPARE—Knocking down all ten pins in two shots.

SPLIT—A spare leave in which the head pin is down and the remaining combination of pins has a gap between them, ranging from the 4–5 to the 7–10.

SPOT—A target on the lane surface at which the bowler aims, ranging from a dot to an arrow to a board or area.

STANCE—The balanced starting position that bowlers assume before making their approach and delivery.

STRIKE—Knocking down all ten pins on the first ball.

STRIKING OUT—Finishing the game with a string of consecutive strikes

STRING—A number of continuous strikes.

STROKER—A bowling style that relies on being smooth and accurate creating only a minimal amount of hook.

SWEEPER—1) A form of competition that usually is conducted in association with another tournament. 2) A separate competition at the end of a league.

SYNTHETIC LANE—A nonwood or manmade lane surface that may be placed over an existing wood lane or a preconstructed unit placed on a foundation.

SYNTHETIC PINS—Nonwood or manmade pins.

Bowling primarily is a team sport enjoyed by up to five players.

T

TAP—A single pin that stands on a seemingly perfect strike shot.

TARGET—A mark or area of the lane the bowler uses to aim his or her shot.

TARGETING—Selecting a spot on the lane for the ball to roll over, such as the dots, the arrows, or a particular board or area. Some bowlers select the pins.

TEAM USA—The official USBC team composed of men and women representing the United States in international competition.

TIMING—A measurement of where the ball is in relationship to the steps during the approach.

TOURNAMENT—A competition where bowlers or teams compete in a single or series of events against all others in their division.

TURKEY—Three consecutive strikes.

U

UNITED STATES BOWLING CONGRESS—The organization created when the American Bowling Congress, Women's International Bowling Congress, Young American Bowling Alliance, and USA Bowling merged into one organization on January 1, 2005.

URETHANE—A material used in making the cover of a bowling ball.

USA BOWLING—Formerly recognized by the U.S. Olympic Committee as the organization responsible for amateur competition in the United States.

USBC COACHING—Organization headquartered in Arlington, Texas, that trains and certifies coaches to teach the sport of bowling. USBC Coaching is the only bowling coaching program recognized by the U.S. Olympic Committee.

W

WIBC—Women's International Bowling Congress, one of four organizations that merged to form the United States Bowling Congress on January 1, 2005.

WOOD LANE—A lane constructed from maple and pine.

Y

YABA—Young American Bowling Alliance, one of four organizations that merged to form the USBC on January 1, 2005.

NOTE: *This lexicon was provided by the United States Bowling Congress.*

INDEX